best seat in the house
cats in their windows

text and photographs by marcie jan bronstein
foreword by tracie hotchner

With gratitude:
to the kind cat owners who welcomed me into their homes
and to Lindsay, book lover, cat lover (Puffy, Frisky, Fatty), and
generous friend, who pointed me in the right direction
and finally to Billy Collins for allowing me to reprint the beginning of his
beautiful poem "Monday" . . . glowing inspiration for this book.
— mjb

Published by Sellers Publishing, Inc.

Copyright © 2009 Marcie Jan Bronstein
All rights reserved.

Sellers Publishing, Inc., P.O. Box 818, Portland, Maine 04104
For ordering information: toll free (800) 625-3386, fax (207) 772-6814
Visit our Web site: www.sellerspublishing.com • E-mail: rsp@rsvp.com

ISBN: 13: 978-1-4162-0531-9

10 9 8 7 6 5 4 3 2 1

Printed and bound in China.

foreword

For many years I had a house called La Fonte in the farmland of Tuscany where I rescued three tiny feral kittens. I named them Rosso, Grigio, and Bianca (after their red, gray, and white colors) and although skittish, they came to enjoy human companionship and spending time inside the warm, dry farmhouse. I was a part-time resident in La Fonte, so I would only see the kitties during the summers, the month of Christmas, and often at Easter (a nice farmer's wife looked after them and the house when I wasn't there). Yet always upon my return, after driving past sunflower and wheat fields and the spring that gave the house its name, nothing punctuated "coming home" like the vision of those three pussycat faces in the window, framed by wooden shutters.

Those cats made a "sometime house" into a home for me. As Marcie Jan Bronstein has so beautifully expressed, in images and in words, my cats were like sentinels, keeping the home fires burning, patiently waiting and watching from their proverbial catbird's seat in the window. The painted photographs in this wonderful book celebrate the mystery and majesty of the cats in our lives by showcasing them within the light-filled frames of their windows.

tracie hotchner

introduction

Cats are like actors who really want to be directors. And to their credit, that, in all honesty, is what they are. While I was fully responsible for writing the text and composing each photograph, I could never say that this book was created on my terms. I may have had my ideas and intentions, but in the end, I was at the mercy of the cats.

Unlike dogs, cats cannot be guided and coaxed to engage with the camera. I spent many months photographing cats in their windows, by wandering with my camera, and by going into people's homes. All the while, there were long catless days, walking on street after street, passing by window after empty window, when I literally told myself out loud that I was crazy to pursue such an elusive and unpredictable subject. Too many times, I'd see a gorgeous cat in a window, and just as I raised my camera to my eye, in a blink she was gone.

Of course that's what this book is all about: cats are not sitting in their windows for our sake. They're there, with their insatiable curiosity, because they know that a window is unquestionably the best seat in the house.

marcie jan bronstein

The birds are in their trees,
the toast is in the toaster,
and the poets are at their windows...

~ from Billy Collins' poem, "Monday"

There are cats in windows alone,

cats in windows with friends,

cats in windows with relatives,

and kittens learning about windows.

There are cats in front of windows,

cats below windows,

cats beside windows,

and cats in boxes in windows.

It's an enviable marriage:
The window frames the cat

and the cat enlivens the window.

One can't help but wonder
if cats know that their presence
makes a building more beautiful,

more compelling,

and more complete.

Maybe that's why you'll find cats in windows
even when there aren't cats in windows.

There's no place like home . . .
and for cats,
there's no place in a home
like a window.

Bathed in a world of light

and warmed by the rays of the sun,

cats are simply and completely
drawn to their windows.

Any kind of window.

Especially custom-made windows.

Because a window for a cat
is so many things . . .
it's a passage

and a mirror,

a seat for traveling
to distant imaginary places

and for traveling to places
that are deep down inside.

Windows are for looking into

and leaning out of.

Windows are for hide-and-seek

and for people watching.

Windows are for waiting and wondering and wishing.

We're welcome
to watch cats watching us
from their windows,

but cats have rules about personal space.

Though most don't seem to mind
sharing their windows,

some appear to have opinions about the decor.

Nevertheless,
interior design doesn't really matter.

Cats are focused
on the wild, open world outside . . .

where the views have no boundaries,

and where one can't possibly imagine what might happen . . .

from one moment to the next.

The whole endeavor can be rather tiring . . .

even utterly exhausting.

Fortunately,
cats know when it's time to take a break.

And they know when it's time to return.

After all, cats play so many roles:
They are sphinxes,
ancient guards protecting their homes.

They are your neighbors,
keeping their eyes on you.

Cats, like photographers, are voyeurs

and possibly even spies.

Cats, without a doubt,
see dimensions of you

that you have never seen yourself.

So what can we learn from our cats?

That each new sunrise

shining through a light-filled frame

is only the beginning
of a day
just waiting
to be met.